A Heart Awake
TO Beauty

Nature's Influence Upon the Soul

DEE APPEL   *Art by* MARK KEATHLEY

BLUE COTTAGE GIFTS
a division of Multnomah Publishers, Inc.
Sisters, Oregon

A Heart Awake to Beauty
Copyright ©2001 by Dee Appel
Published by Blue Cottage Gifts™, a division of Multnomah Publishers, Inc.®
P.O. Box 1720, Sisters, Oregon 97759

ISBN 1-58860-025-4

Artwork by Mark Keathley is reproduced with permission from Newmark Publishing
USA. For prints of the artwork, please contact:

Newmark Publishing USA
11700 Commonwealth Drive
Louisville, Kentucky 40299
1-800-866-5566

Designed by Koechel Peterson & Associates, Minneapolis, Minnesota

Multnomah Publishers, Inc., has made every effort to trace the ownership of all poems
and quotes. In the event of a question arising from the use of a poem or quote, we regret
any error made and will be pleased to make the necessary correction in future editions
of this book.

Scripture quotations are taken from *The Holy Bible*, New International Version ©1973,
1984 by International Bible Society, used by permission of Zondervan Publishing House;
The Holy Bible, King James Version (KJV); Revised Standard Version Bible (RSV) ©1946,
1952 by the Division of Christian Education of the National Council of the Churches
of Christ in the United States of America.

Printed in China

01 02 03 04 05 06—10 9 8 7 6 5 4 3 2 1 0

www.bluecottagegifts.com

DEDICATION

With thanks and love to my Dayspring "family," especially those who have hung out with me in the wilderness, singing by campfires under the open skies of the Eagle Cap range. To Skip and Carol, for all their support, from spiritual to financial. To Lon and Ronda, who have generously shared their little piece of heaven known to me as Melody Mountain. Always to my children, Jennifer, Erik, and Nikolas. I pray that you will all continue to bask in the wonder of the great outdoors. And to my grandchildren, present and future. May you grow to treasure the boundless beauty God has gifted to us in nature.

TABLE OF CONTENTS

A Heart Awake to Beauty 6

Spring: Majestic Mountain Melody 12

Heart of the Meadow 18

Summer: Gems of the Morning—Dewdrops 24

Brookside Soliloquy 28

Songbird's Lullaby 32

A Quiet Place 36

Fall: Blush of Autumn 40

Cathedrals in the Forest 44

Timberline Twilight 48

Winter: The Hush of Winter.....................................54

Moonlight Reverie..58

A HEART AWAKE
TO BEAUTY

*Nature's Influence
upon the Soul*

*Nature is the
living, visible
garment of God.*

GOETHE

Every morning I awaken to beautiful birds at the feeders outside my bedroom window. I share their delight as the sun splashes onto the golden oak trees framing the land that has been my view for nearly twenty-five years. Whenever I do wander from home, it is simply to immerse myself in nature in some other glorious form, usually mountains and high lakes. I have always found in nature my soul's restoration and a deep and abiding wonder at God's incredible artwork. Violet and lavender sunsets airbrushed in an indigo sky. Great mirrored lakes that leave me breathless as they reflect near-perfect images of jagged mountain peaks. Carved in stark relief against the horizon, an occasional elk or deer wandering past.

For those of us who are rejuvenated by the rhythm of nature, we cannot fathom a world otherwise orchestrated. Some do not hear what we hear. Strains of a violin, like gossamer wings, whisper to our soul, transporting us to another dimension. Sunrise has its own symphony, as does the harvest moon, hung in fiery suspension on an early autumn eve. There is no silence. There is merely a different performance by the orchestra.

The pan flute calls hauntingly in the falling rain. Tom-toms of thunder ricochet through canyons as lightning splits the heavy summer sky. The gentle touch of a morning breeze stirs the reeds of a piccolo. Even harsh winter winds, discordant though they may be, carry their own song. The sweet notes of the meadow's lark pluck the strings of our heart's own harp, welcoming the dawning of a new day. Spindly-legged fawns are birthed on dew-laden spring grasses to the cellist's concerto.

Chords of golden harmonies wrap themselves around an afternoon rainbow, twisting and curling like wisteria clinging to the garden trellis. The eagle, sky-swimming in the depth of summer, moves in accordance with nature's own melodies. She cloaks herself, season by season, in rare and radiant garments and offers up the rhythms of her unending song.

And nestled in the robes of nature's glory we find her most prized treasures. She instructs us. She speaks to us of life imparting a message about its fundamental simplicity. She speaks to us of seasons, reminding us that our lives have seasons of their own. She speaks in a voice of soft mornings and gentle evenings, a voice sweetened by the fragrance of wild mint that flourishes beside the still waters.

Welcome to this celebration of nature in all her finery. May you draw from the ageless wisdom she offers you.

❧

If eyes were made for seeing,
Then beauty is its own excuse for being.

RALPH WALDO EMERSON

Heard melodies are sweet, but those unheard are sweeter...

JOHN KEATS

The Treasures of Nature

Nature holds the secrets and
The treasures of the earth:
Her seasons teach of days renewed,
Of death, and life, and birth.
Sometimes her ways are strong and harsh,
As life can be for man,
But respite comes as spring will, too,
Relieving time's demands.

There's so much wisdom we can glean
When we turn eyes to see.
She gladly shares her wares with us…
Unfolds her mysteries.
Breathe deeply of her heady scents
And amble down her trails.
Relief resides for you and me…
Simplicity prevails.

MAJESTIC MOUNTAIN MELODY

A Cause to Rejoice

Go forth under the open sky, and listen to Nature's teachings.

WILLIAM CULLEN BRYANT

Many of us have a special place of respite. Perhaps yours is a closely-guarded secret. No one knows about your very own spot, accessed only by an overgrown road that winds its way into the deep pine woods. Or perhaps you don your hiking shoes and head for higher ground and a refreshing pool at the base of a waterfall that gushes from the mountainside. Or maybe your destination is not so much the source of solace as the "getting there" is.

There is a place I go whenever life's demands become more than I can bear. I hurry there like some creature under serious scrutiny by its predator. There I find relief and my soul's restoration. Weariness falls from me as I begin my ascent. The mountain's majestic peaks rise before me and her magnificence raises my spirit.

The air is fine and gloriously fresh. The mornings are long and lazy. I have visited in every season, even tromping up her foothills on frozen nights, breaking through the top crust of the snow beneath my feet and sinking into the marshmallow softness below. On those winter hikes, I always arrive breathless and rosy-cheeked to stand awestruck under a sky so brilliant that tears seem the most natural, and only appropriate, response to its splendor.

Each breath I draw as I stand in this sanctuary nurtures me, calms me, blesses me. Being there causes me to pause and give thanks for life itself, and so it can be for you. Take a moment to reflect upon the important things in your life—family, children, faith, health. We forget that we cannot live life one second faster, regardless of how we may try. And life is so much better if we don't try, if we stop our running. Carving out moments of time to visit our places of respite can remind us of the importance of slowing down. And we need to be reminded because we change and move and leave behind those sacred places and those holy moments of insight and the perspective they provide. But knowing that they await our return gives us cause to rejoice!

To him who in the love of Nature holds communion with her visible forms, she speaks a various language.

WILLIAM CULLEN BRYANT

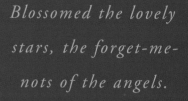

Blossomed the lovely stars, the forget-me-nots of the angels.

HENRY WADSWORTH
LONGFELLOW

Song of the Mountain

Jagged peaks this mountain shape.
They rise from valleys low
To touch the hem of gold-lined clouds
That softly, gently flow.
And deep within her heart beats still
The rhythm of her song.
She's wooed by Wolf and Nightingale
That to her alone belong.

Her song is one of ancient days;
It rises and it fades.
It carries velvet colors there
From amethyst to jade,
The song will linger on the night
The moon will wax and wane
Then rise beyond majestic peak
To hear her song again.

SPRING:
HEART OF
THE MEADOW

Perpetual Hope

You will be

secure, because

there is hope.

JOB 11:18

By the time winter reaches its soggy end in Oregon where I live, I am so ready for spring I can barely stand it. It is hard to describe how I long for the sun to warm me, heart and soul. It is really rather ironic that I was born and raised in Oregon and have now reared a family of my own here as well. The Pacific Northwest is not known for its warm, dry climate. People joke about the webs between our toes and that the "tans" we sport are really rust. Sometimes those statements seem not far from the truth. Oregon pays a wet price for the lush coat she wears!

Like my beloved Oregon, each one of us experiences times in our lives that feel like a long, desolate, and unending winter. We yearn for the hope of spring and all it represents. Whether we have gone through illness (our own or a loved one's), divorce, or death—with whatever the loss, there comes a time when we cry out for relief. And that relief, like spring itself, inevitably appears, often just when we need it the most.

In our lives, spring arrives at varying times and wearing different faces. Sometimes spring comes in the dead of winter in the form of a freshly cut bouquet sent by someone who loves us. Sometimes spring is disguised as a warm berry pie prepared by a dear neighbor. Or it comes with the discovery, on an early frigid morn, of a crocus peeking out to see if it is safe to bloom.

Spring arrives late in the heart of a mountain meadow. Sometimes at higher elevations, you will find daffodils and wild lilacs as late as July. Velvet carpets of color sweep over her gently sloping shoulders, their hues chosen from a palette unlike any other. The meadow gathers her skirts of heather and lupine around her. And like a young woman dressing for a first date, she bathes herself in the sweet scents of spring.

Such comfort comes in knowing that, regardless of the severity of our winter, spring will come! It may come early, as it does in the valley, or it might be delayed, as it is in the heart of a mountain meadow, but it will arrive. That truth should give us perpetual hope.

❧

Whoever has a mind that is free, may go forth to the fields and to the woods, inhaling joyous renovation from the breath of Spring, or catching the odors and sounds of Autumn some diviner mood of sweetest sadness, which improves the softened heart.

PERCY BYSSHE SHELLEY

❧

Not knowing when the dawn will come, I open every door.

EMILY DICKINSON

A BREATH OF SPRING

Springtime takes her first warm breath

And gently lets it go.

It stirs green shoots below the crust

Of winter's last-seen snow.

Each day awakes to sweetened air

That's filled with hope renewed.

It washes clean the last remains

Of winter's attitude.

New life is born beside fresh fields

Of clover and young heather.

Here a sow instructs her young

As they play together.

Tucked far away, no eye may see

This rhythmic song sublime.

The meadow keeps a secret

That withstands the test of time.

SUMMER:
GEMS OF THE
MORNING —
DEWDROPS

A Good Place to Start

*Everything in
Nature contains
all the powers
of Nature.*

RALPH WALDO EMERSON

Just before a summer's dawn, the world is deeply silent. Nature slips on her rainbow apron, studded with dewy gems of the morning, and prepares to greet the day. As the sun peeks over hill and vale, vermilion streaks stretch along the sweeping horizon, as the sun peeks over hill and vale, tearing loose from the night it leaves behind, vermilion streaks stretch along the sweeping horizon. Tentacles of warmth begin to reach through the valleys, bringing the day into view.

Sunshine brings thoughts of life in full swing. Of freshly-washed clothes hanging in multi-color along a backyard line. Long furrows carved in the soil, waiting to embrace the farmer's life-bearing seeds. Uninvited weeds mocking the hard-working gardener. Or of lazy days of back porch swinging, barbecues, and afternoon swims. Of sitting around campfires singing "Kum-bayah My Lord" and "Michael, Row the Boat Ashore."

One of the first songs I learned to sing in the 1950s was "Mockingbird Hill." Something about the lyrics of the song touched my spirit, foreshadowing the person I would become. Sweet and lilting in melody, the song tells of the morning sun peeking over the hill to kiss the roses on "my windowsill." Even today this happy song brings a smile to my face. I have continued to sing it through the years, first to my own children and now to my grandchildren. Its lines remind me of less complicated ways and simpler times: "Got a horse and a plow and an old whippoorwill…." The words have encouraged questions from my little ones. Their interest provides opportunity to sow seeds of basic values and to strengthen young virtue. We have to start somewhere. And just as morning begins each new day, this song has given me a place to start teaching my children important lessons for life.

*While the morning
stars sang together
and all the angels
shouted for joy.*

JOB 38:7

❧

I'll tell you how the sun rose—

A ribbon at a time

The steeples swam in amethyst

The news like squirrels ran.

The hills untied their bonnets,

The bobolinks begun.

Then I said softly to myself,

"That must have been the sun."

EMILY DICKINSON

🐝

BROOKSIDE SOLILOQUY

The Secret Is Laughter

Sweet are the little
brooks that run
O'er pebbles
glancing in the
sun, singing in
soothing tones.

THOMAS HOOD

There is nothing like the sound of a brook. Burbling. Babbling. Buffeting. Trickling. Tripping. Tumbling. Skipping. Leaping. Lapping. Sliding. Hiding. Dribbling. Drifting. Splashing. It murmurs to itself by day and by night. And it laughs. Repeatedly. Continuously. Happily keeping company with the salamanders and tadpoles. They tickle its tummy, causing hopeless, helpless, uninterrupted bliss.

My youngest grandson is only a year-and-a-half old, but he has a gurgling laugh that is completely infectious. He walks around with a look that says, "I know something you don't..." I personally think it has to do with what he sees of the world. It's a simple view we adults too soon forget. Doorknobs and elevator buttons. Knees and unmatched socks. Untied shoes and pebbles on the ground. A child's perspective is definitely uncomplicated. A carefree child reminds me of the little brook...flowing happily down the mountainside...knowing something we don't know...and enjoying the complete effortlessness of it all.

Today people create their own creeks by using electric pumps to circulate water through their little garden waterfalls. Clay statues of lovely maidens water clay flowers; concrete reproductions of waterwheel houses lazily push water to the next level. This scramble to create the sound of moving water in our backyards may be a quest for its soothing properties.

Think about the almost immediate and instinctive response when we sit down beside a bubbling creek. It seems natural to unfurl a checkered tablecloth and retrieve some luscious grapes and a hunk of cheese from the picnic basket...to untie our shoes and bury our toes in the silt at the welcoming edges of the water...or to try to perform an amateur balancing act as we attempt cross the creek without slipping off the mossy rocks. Are these simple pleasures a brief return to a time in our lives when we knew the secrets?

Perhaps when life is getting to be a bit much we ought to stare at knees and socks and doorknobs. Or pack a picnic lunch. The secret they share is laughter.

I'd like to be a boy again, a care-free prince of joy again,
I'd like to tread the hills and dales the way I used to do;
I'd like the tattered shirt again, the knickers thick with dirt again,
The ugly, dusty feet again that long ago I knew.
I'd like to play first base again, and Sliver's curves to face again,
I'd like to climb, the way I did, a friendly apple tree;
For, knowing what I do to-day, could I but wander back and play,
I'd get full measure of the joy that boy-hood gave to me.

EDGAR A. GUEST, "THE WISH"

To laugh often and much; to win the respect of intelligent people and the affection of children...to appreciate beauty, to find the best in others; to leave the world a little better.

RALPH WALDO EMERSON

SONGBIRD'S LULLABY

A Song of Thanksgiving

There is a turning point at day's end—a place where afternoon meets evening. The wind may pick up just a bit. Or it may calm. The sky takes on the slightest tinge of pink. In summer, the air is heavy. Or arid. Or sticky. The earth is ready for relief. Birds of prey have filled their bellies and, like children holding out for one more game of hide and seek, they soar their last few moments on the day's thermals.

Shadows begin to seep from behind great boulders. Certain flowers fold their petals inward, as if in supplication.

As nature takes a deep breath and prepares to close her eyes, the pure, sweet song of a lark or nightingale arises. The lullaby begins…sung from a heart unfettered by worldly worry or care. Sung for the pure joy of it. Sung to the trees and the beasts and the carpets of wildflowers. Sung in thanksgiving. Sung with clarity and purpose. The notes are lifted to the heavens, offered as a gift of love without expectation of receiving anything in return.

We can find this same joy if we dare. If we look for the good in life, in people, and in circumstances, we can find our voice. It isn't always easy, but it is possible. Perhaps our expectations of what we might or should get in return hold us back and keep us from giving. I believe life returns to us what we freely give…like a circle, it completes itself. When, for instance, we offer help to one another, without agenda, without thought of reciprocation,we reap the blessings. And inevitably others come alongside us when we are in need. That pattern is worthy of our thanksgiving. Worthy of our effort. Taking a lesson from the lark, we, too, could end each day with a song.

EVENSONG

Sing your song, oh feathered one!

Lift it to the sky!

Fluff your pinions in the wind

As night comes drifting by.

Bless the flowers and the trees,

Bless the clouds up high.

Tuck us in tonight, we pray,

To a songbird's lullaby.

❦

The Lord is my strength and my
shield.... My heart leaps for joy and I
will give thanks to him in song.

PSALM 28:7

❦

A thing of beauty is a
joy forever; it's loveliness
increases; it will never
pass into nothingness.

JOHN KEATS

A QUIET PLACE

Importance of Solitude

> *I have never found a companion that was so companionable as solitude.*
>
> HENRY DAVID THOREAU

Like a child blowing dandelion puffs, the wind breathes gently across the water's surface, stirring the softest of ripples. Bits of feathers float past, left behind by mama ducks or geese who have lined their nests with the down of their own bellies. Around the pond, grasses grow in lush patches, leaning into one another in fond embrace.

Have you ever knelt down beside a pond like that and watched the activity above and beneath its surface? Once a stream bubbling with life, the water has stopped here, becoming in a moment of respite a gloriously calm pool. Regrouping. Redirecting. Reconnecting. The still waters somehow draw us to a place of peace and solace with its unsung song.

I used to be afraid to be alone, and the fear was probably a carryover from my childhood. Since I was an only child, my parents often had to import playmates for me. But somehow I translated their actions into the message "It's not okay to be alone." And I carried that thought around in my adult self for a long time. Then one day I discovered the splendor of solitude. I think it happened when some angel took my three children and I got to have an uninterrupted bath! I discovered the unbridled joy of quiet moments. The sweetness of uninterrupted thoughts. The blessed relief of being alone and still.

Each of us needs to find quiet places in our lives. We rush too hurriedly through our days and nights, adding more and more projects and activities. Getting through the day's demands drains us of our physical strength and our emotional resources and we find it more and more difficult to slow down the pace.

But even a river rushing down a mountainside eventually settles into a deep, calm pool or stretches out into long, lazy patches. In fact, the waters often run deepest there. I think it is seeking solitude. Enjoying its own company.

Long, lazy patches in life are important. Enjoying our own company is good.

OF DEEPEST WORTH

These are the things I prize
And hold of deepest worth:
Light of the sapphire skies,
Peace of the silent hills,
Shelter of forest, comfort of the grass,
Shadow of clouds that swiftly pass,

And after showers
The smell of flowers,
And of the good brown earth—
And best of all, along the way,
Friendship and mirth.

HENRY VAN DYKE

This is the place.
Stand still, my
steed—Let me
review the scene,
And summon from
the shadowy past
the forms that once
have been.

HENRY WADSWORTH
LONGFELLOW

FALL:
A HARVEST
OF WISDOM

A Blush of Autumn

Oh, tenderly the

haughty day

Fills his blue urn

with fire.

RALPH WALDO EMERSON

Stands of aspen flicker in the wind as leaves flecked with silver and gold watch autumn steal summer's end. Cirrus clouds wisp their way across cobalt skies. Earth ripens to its fullest. Velveteen hills and fields of sage and sienna turn chocolate behind the farmer's plow. And sunlight dances through leaves blazing gloriously in shades of vermilion.

If I had to pick a favorite season, it would definitely be early autumn. Here in Oregon we are often blessed with Indian summers, those days of extraordinary golden splendor plus a taste of warmth still on their breath. Days when you can nap in your hammock if you can get away with it. Days when you build a fire in the woodstove to take the chill off the morning, or afternoons perfect for raking leaves and jumping in the pile. Fall evenings with crisp hints of the coolness to come. Harvested fields that have yielded their bounty, feeding, blessing, prompting heartfelt thanks.

Likewise, in the autumn of our lives, we are to have ripened in wisdom. Ideally the summers of our youth give way to an understanding that comes only from life experience, from the accumulation of instruction and training. We are moving toward a season that allows us to share our harvest gifts, a bounty of hard-won wisdom, a heart humbled by life's journey, and a contentment that comes with both. There is a definite sweetness in this harvest.

Ah! Sweet September

Fall arrives on summer's wings

And steals her warmest ways;

Blazing colors mark the hour

At dawning's first-lit haze.

Misty morns swirl 'neath oak

To rise in later rays

And pay respect to what is left

Of summer's long-lost days.

❧

The day becomes more solemn and serene

When noon is past—there is harmony

In Autumn, and a lustre in its sky,

Which through the summer is not heard or seen,

As if it could not be, as if it had not been!

PERCY BYSSHE SHELLEY

Knowledge comes,
but wisdom lingers.

ALFRED LORD TENNYSON

CATHEDRALS IN THE FOREST

Lessons of Life

*Of all the man's
works of art, a
cathedral is the
greatest. A vast and
majestic tree is
greater than that.*

HENRY WARD BEECHER

Hidden in the cleft of a mountain pass in Eastern Oregon, as if clutched protectively to its breast, sits the patchwork cabin that holds my heart. Slanting floors and falling-down ceilings. No indoor "facilities." No running water. But if I step outside the door, I can lower a bucket into the antique structure that houses an artesian well, pull up a bucket of mountain nectar, and drink from its pure, clear reservoir. Here I sit on rustic furniture and write to my heart's content.

Surrounded by leaded windowpanes that creakily open outward to a cathedral beauty like none other, I am free to experience life at a more leisurely pace. I can reflect on its changes and consider how they will affect me. The fragrance of pine trees wafts in, mingling with the aroma of my morning coffee (there is electricity). I stop and listen to the forest, for there is much to learn here....

It has been an unusually extreme forest fire season in the West this year. I am always saddened to hear of heavily wooded acreage that is decimated by out-of-control infernos. Yet I have learned that certain new growth can only occur in the aftermath of such a fire. Some tree pods are actually activated in the wake of these blazes. Also, forests are amazingly able to spring back from ashy-black ruins. And within a short time, it is difficult to see the scars of the devastation.

Sometimes, like forests, our lives are touched by fire, perhaps not literally, but certainly figuratively. And even if the flames don't burn dramatically, they nevertheless sear our hearts. Think about those passages of life when we are obliged to go forward despite the smoke and the heat. Growing up. Moving.

Changing jobs. Aging. Seeing children leave the nest.

All of these can mean upheaval, and all of them leave an aftermath of emotion. But changes like these often teach us the most, stretch us the farthest. And the new growth they spawn gives us a fresh perspective on our lives and new appreciation for its gifts.

Fire is part of the life cycle's rhythm. And just as fires in the woods are often key to the reforestation, so the fiery circumstances of life are key to our growth.

THE SENTINELS

Amongst the boughs and branches
Of the redwoods and the birch,
Trapped within their aged rings,
Are stories of the earth.

Standing firm and rooted,
With many or with few,
They've tasted winter's frigid tongue
And kissed spring's morning dew.

Each evening they attend the rites…
The setting of the sun
As it rests within the foothills
When summer's day is done.

The trees retain the cadence
Of nature's simplest sound.
They weave and sway and echo back
With eloquent resound.

Those green-robed
senators of
mighty woods,
Tall oaks,
branch-charmed
by the earnest stars,
Dream, and so
dream all night
without stir.

JOHN KEATS

TIMBERLINE
TWILIGHT

Captured Moments in Time

Photographers love that time just after sunset when a gentle glow adds softness to the earth's sometimes harsh lines. This magical twilight time is known as "the golden hour." In my office at home hangs a lovely photo of Mt. Hood taken at just that moment. The trees are so snow-laden that their hidden shape is almost an illusion. Cotton-candy clouds etched in filigree hover over the 11,000 foot summit. The glacier blushes in the afterglow of the day, like cheeks on a running child who has just come in for dinner. You can almost step into the quietude of the moment. And sometimes I do step into that tranquility....

Hold the fleet
angel fast until he
bless thee.

HENRY WADSWORTH
LONGFELLOW

Likewise, various seasons of our lives offer windows of opportunity to step into the serenity of twilight, to be bathed in the softness of a golden hour. These chances are often once-in-a-lifetime, freeze-frame moments.

I recall one such scene from long years ago. One late afternoon I looked out across the cattails and crotchety apple trees to the old railway bed and caught sight of my flaxen-haired son, then about eight, as he ran flat-out with our yellow lab close on his heels. Completely oblivious to any other thing in his life, he was utterly delighting in the joy of being an eight-year-old. Time stopped. I captured him there in that very second. And though the lab is no longer with us and the child today hovers over me at six feet four inches, I can forever return to that twilight moment.

It is good to seek the "golden hours," the golden moments, of our lives. They can slip away all too easily and become "if-only's." So capture them as they come by. They are worthy of being seized. And, once seized, these frozen moments are worthy of our repeated visits. They stay there, soft in line and bathed in a gentle glow, engraved in their twilight time.

❧

Sundown is the hour for many strange effects
in light and shade—enough to make a
colorist go delirious—long spokes of molten
silver sent horizontally through the trees
(now in their brightest, tenderest green),
each leaf and branch of endless foliage a
lit-up miracle, then lying all prone on the
youthful-ripe, interminable grass, and giving
the blades not only aggregate but individual
splendor, in ways unknown to any other hour.

WALT WHITMAN

❧

*Day's sweetest
moments are
at dawn.*

ELLA WHEELER WILCOX

O Gift of God! O Perfect day;
Whereon shall no man work, but play;
Whereon it is enough for me,
Not to be doing, but to be!

Through every fibre of my brain,
Through every nerve, through every vein,
I feel the electric thrill, the touch
Of life, that seems almost too much.

I hear the wind among the trees
Playing celestial symphonies;
I see the branches downward bent,
Like keys of some great instrument.

And over me unrolls on high
The splendid scenery of the sky,
Where through a sapphire sea the sun
Sails like a golden galleon…

O Life and Love! O happy throng
Of thoughts, whose only speech is song!
O heart of man! Canst thou not be
Blithe as the air is, and as free!

HENRY WADSWORTH LONGFELLOW

WINTER:
THE HUSH OF WINTER

The Final Cycle

*For he saith to
the snow, Be
thou on the
earth.... By the
breath of God
frost is given.*

JOB 37:6,10, KJV

*W*inter, wrapped in ermine and diamonds, arrives somehow unexpectedly at our doorstep. Cedar logs crackle at the hearth as children press their noses against windowpanes and beg to be released. Outside, they roll in snowbanks, losing themselves in the sparkling wonderland. Lying on their backs, they stick their tongues out and taste snowflakes one by one. Or they flap their "wings," leaving angel impressions behind. Their laughter tinkles in the frosty air.

In the mountains, winter does not come quietly. It swoops in like an eagle snatching its prey. Suddenly the jagged peaks are softened by mounds of white fluff. Frigid nights give way to crisp dawnings where our breath is captured in clouds as it leaves us in conversation. As the weeks pass, huge drifts grow in both height and breadth. Glaciers expand and dig in for the season. Wildlife seeks sustenance from the mountain's meager remains. Winter winds wail through canyons.

Even so, the coming of winter brings a unique kind of comfort. It's the comfort of dormancy and hibernation, of rest and recovery. Yet often we associate winter with endings. The last of the seasons. The end of a year. Even, metaphorically, the end of a life. Last winter was my mother's last. As autumn faded, so did her health. The year's final season began. Ninety-four winters. She was birthed in harder, but simpler times. She delivered me later in life than most women of her era. She often commented that, for her, life began at forty. She lived to watch her three grandchildren grow up and to hold two great-grandchildren in her arms. Winter last year—for her as well as for me—was an ending. In the quiet of the night, in the depth of winter, she was gone. And there was peace in her going. Comfort in the release of a life lived fully and with grace.

So, layer by layer, winter drapes itself over hill and mountain. Each new snowfall muffles more and more the sounds and movements of life until some nights seem so silent and still you can hear the moon's heartbeat. The hush has fallen. Peace has arrived.

Similarly, layer by layer, life drapes itself over us. Each of us will have a last winter. Just as the season builds to this finality, so it is with us.

❧

December 15, 1856: I still recall to mind that characteristic winter eve...oak leaves, bleached and withered weeds that rose above the snow, the now dark green of the pines, and perchance the faint metallic chip of a single tree sparrow; the hushed stillness of the wood at sundown, aye, all the winter day; the short boreal twilight; the smooth serenity and the reflections of the pond, still alone free from ice; the melodious hooting of the owl, heard at the same time with the yet more distant whistle of a locomotive...the gilded bar of cloud across the apparent outlet of the pond.

HENRY DAVID THOREAU

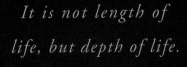

It is not length of life, but depth of life.

RALPH WALDO EMERSON

MOONLIGHT REVERIE

Follow Your Dreams

Go confidently in the direction of your dreams. Live the life you have imagined.

HENRY DAVID THOREAU

Moonlight weaves itself through silhouetted trees and peeks between the leaves, casting its cool radiance over the darkened land as it moves across the starry firmament. Sometimes reflecting its daytime nemesis, it burnishes orange in a harvest sky. Lingering in the company of comets and meteors, stirring tales of cows and spoons, its happy face and plump cheeks bring out the child in us. Its unending cycle is reassuring. Wax and wane. Consistency and cadence. Beginning and end.

When I was young, I dreamed a certain dream several times. We lived on a lake, and in the dream I was standing on the balcony just outside my second-story bedroom door. Suddenly, I had wings. I would fly out across the lake, soaring in the sky, sailing on the wind, and waving to people I knew and loved. Although that particular dream disappeared with adulthood, I can clearly recall even today the feeling it evoked.

Growing up we all have our dreams and aspirations, our high hopes for futures as astronauts, nurses, firefighters, police officers, or perhaps even president of the United States. But as we grow, our dreams may take on a different face. Just as the moon moves from crescent to full, the ambitions and goals of our youth may change. A few of us know the joy of fulfilling the dreams of our childhood. Others of us find contentment and pleasure in reshaping and then realizing our dreams.

Whichever group we find ourselves in, it is good to continue both to dream and to pursue our hopes despite trials and false starts. Oh, some dreams will wax and wane. But others will shine and glow in the fullness of achievement like a pond in the flush of moonlit radiance. Those dreams fulfilled will remind us of happy nights ideal for dancing under the stars, of the childhood joy of roasting marshmallows by the bonfire, or gleefully competing to see who could catch the most fireflies.

The new moon will rise. Victorious and fresh and pristine. And with each new rising comes the promise of future dreams.

❧

The day is done, and the darkness
Falls from the wings of Night,
As a feather is wafted downward
From an eagle in his flight.

HENRY WADSWORTH LONGFELLOW

☙

The moon is distant
from the sea,
And yet with
amber hands
She leads him in,
docile as a boy,
Along appointed sands

EMILY DICKINSON

Moontones

If the moon were an instrument, what would it be?

A pure, gentle oboe lilting over the sea?

Would it be a harp with tones soft and clear

That spin their own tales when the summer is near…

And reach for the earth with most tender strains…

Blushing in autumn with harvest's refrains?

Or tinkling wind chimes
hung there by the door

Reflecting the whispers of nature's own lore?

Would it be the drumbeat of heaven's sweet heart

That echoes its rhythm as it has from the start?

Perhaps you hear cello, piano, or bass

When winter's beheld in its shimmering face

Or the strings of the dulcimer's light harmony

Which speak now that springtime will soon
be set free…

A heaven-hewn instrument created to be

Held in the sky by a hand we don't see—

The Maestro directs it to watch over thee.